Pebble® Plus

> DESTRUCTION <

KNOCK IT DOWN!

by Thomas Kingsley Troupe

Consulting Editor: Gail Saunders-Smith, PhD

CAPSTONE PRESS
a capstone imprint

Pebble Plus is published by Capstone Press,
1710 Roe Crest Drive, North Mankato, Minnesota 56003
www.capstonepub.com

Library of Congress Cataloging-in-Publication Data
Troupe, Thomas Kingsley.
  Knock it down! / by Thomas Kingsley Troupe.
    p. cm.—(Pebble plus. Destruction)
  Audience: 006-008.
  Audience: K to grade 3.
  Summary: "Large, colorful photos and simple text illustrate a structure being knocked down by a wrecking ball and
other machinery"—Provided by publisher.
  Includes bibliographical references and index.
  ISBN 978-1-4765-2087-2 (library binding : alk. paper)—ISBN 978-1-4765-3488-6 (ebook pdf)
1. Wrecking—Juvenile literature. 2. Cranes, derricks, etc.—Juvenile literature. I. Title.
  TH447.T764 2014
  690'.26—dc23   2013002442

Editorial Credits
Erika L. Shores, editor; Heidi Thompson, designer; Marcie Spence, media researcher; Kathy McColley, production specialist

Photo Credits
AP Images: Eric Risberg, 13; Corbis: Martyn Goddard, 9; iStockphoto: ZargonDesign, cover (wrecking ball); Newscom: Bill
Breenblatt, 5, Horst Ossinger Deutsch Presse Agentur, cover, 17, ZUMA Press, 7, 15; Shutterstock: Dheryl Deveney, back
cover, 1, 11, Kevin Day, 21, Rob Kints, 19, VectorZilla, design element

Note to Parents and Teachers

The Destruction set supports social studies standards related to science, technology, and society.
This book describes and illustrates the demolition of structures using a wrecking ball. The images
support early readers in understanding the text. The repetition of words and phrases helps early
readers learn new words. This book also introduces early readers to subject-specific vocabulary
words, which are defined in the Glossary section. Early readers may need assistance to read some
words and to use the Table of Contents, Glossary, Read More, Internet Sites, and Index sections of
the book.

Printed in China by Nordica.
0413/CA21300494
032013   007226NORDF13

Table of contents

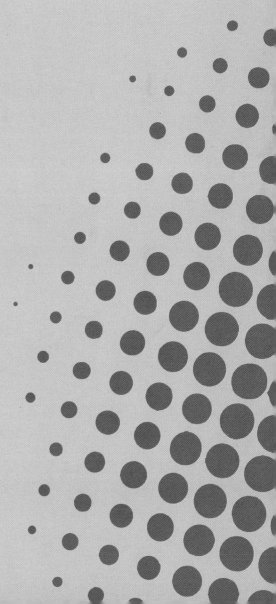

Knock It Down

The old courthouse is

falling apart and dangerous.

5

The demolition crew brings
a crane and heavy vehicles.
The wrecking ball hangs from
a chain on the crane.

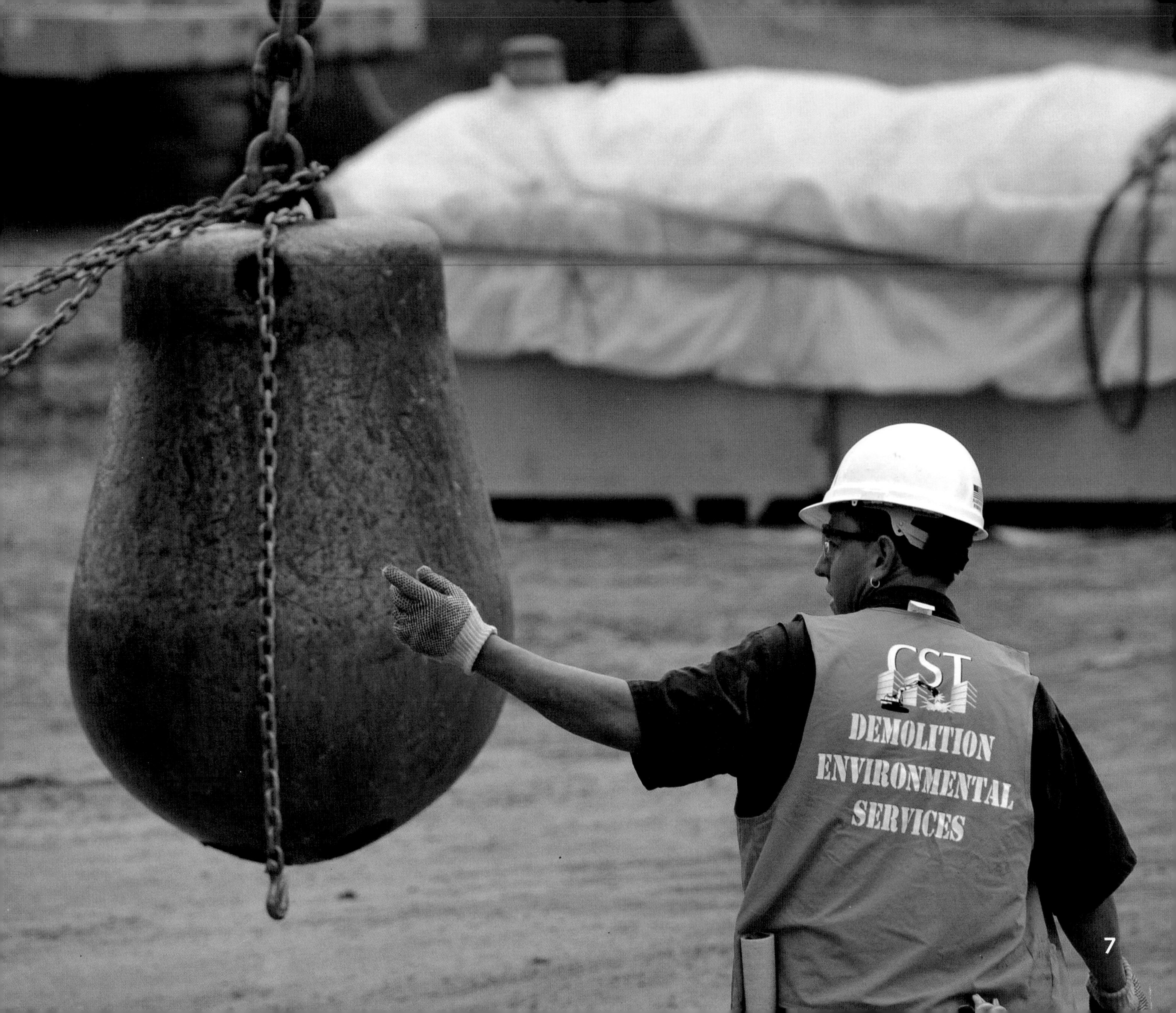
CST
DEMOLITION
ENVIRONMENTAL
SERVICES

Smash It

The crane swings

the wrecking ball and ...

SMASH!

The ball swings again.

11

A worker sprays water on

the smashed building.

It keeps dust from rising.

The building gets

whacked again.

The top floor is knocked
to pieces. Time to bust up
the lower floors!

16

An excavator rips off loose

chunks of the courthouse.

CRUNCH

CRUMBLE

Clean It Up

The crew scoops up the rubble.

They load it into dump trucks.

Now haul it away!

Glossary

crane—a machine with a long arm used to lift and move heavy objects

demolition—the act of destroying something

excavator—a large machine used for digging in the ground or other demolition work

haul—to use a vehicle to move or carry something

rubble—broken bricks, concrete, glass, metal, and other materials left from a building or other structure that has fallen down or been demolished

vehicle—something that carries people or things from place to place

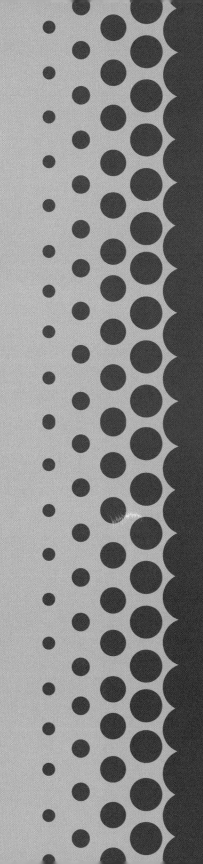